DASH DIET

SOLUTION 2023

The Latest DASH Cookbook With Easy and Delicious Low Sodium Recipes for Healthy Weight Loss and Improve Heart Health

Alice McBride

Table of Contents

INTRODUCTION

As a seasoned Nutritionist, I have witnessed the power of DASH DIET firsthand in improving heart health and healthy weight loss. My Client, Tammy was a 33-year-old mother of two who had *struggled with her weight for years*. She had tried every diet plan out there, from Low-Carb to Keto to Intermittent fasting, but none of them seemed to work for her. She was frustrated and felt like giving up until when she came to me, I knew I had to devise a personalized eating plan to address her unique dietary needs. So I came up with the **"DASH Diet Weight Loss Solution."**

Initially, Tammy was skeptical about the DASH Diet, as she had never heard of it before. However, after trying out some of the recipes I recommend, she was pleasantly surprised. The meals were *delicious, satisfying, and easy to prepare.*

After just a few weeks on the DASH Diet, Tammy started to notice changes in her body. Her clothes were *fitting better, she had more energy, and her blood pressure had improved significantly.* She continued to follow the DASH Diet plan and within a few months, she had *lost over 20 pounds and was feeling better than ever.*

Now, I am thrilled to share my knowledge and expertise with you through my latest cookbook, **"DASH Diet Weight Loss Solution 2023."** This cookbook is an all-encompassing guide that features easy and delicious DASH recipes to aid in healthy weight loss and improve heart health. The DASH diet has been proven to be effective in reducing blood pressure and promoting overall cardiovascular health.

This cookbook contains a range of low sodium ingredients and nutrients that are crucial for maintaining healthy heart function while also promoting weight loss. Every recipe has been verified by a nutritionist and customized to meet the individual dietary needs of those who are looking to improve *their heart health and achieve healthy weight loss on the DASH diet.*

I am grateful that you have chosen my cookbook, and I am confident that the recipes included in this book will guide you to your weight-loss objectives and help you live a healthier and more joyful life.

CHAPTER 1

THE DASH DIET BASIC GUIDE

The DASH diet is a healthy eating plan designed to prevent and lower high blood pressure. It's a well-balanced and flexible eating pattern that emphasizes whole foods, fruits, vegetables, and low-fat dairy products. The DASH diet also recommends reducing sodium, saturated fats, and added sugars.

The DASH diet is based on scientific research and has been shown to help lower blood pressure, improve cholesterol levels, and reduce the risk of heart disease, stroke, and kidney disease. The diet is also effective for weight loss and weight management.

The DASH diet is easy to follow and doesn't require any special foods or supplements. It's based on a daily caloric intake of 2,000 calories, but it can be adjusted to meet individual needs.

The key components of the DASH diet include:

1. Fruits and vegetables: The DASH diet emphasizes a variety of fruits and vegetables, including fresh, frozen, canned, or dried. These are rich in vitamins, minerals, and fiber.

2. Whole grains: The DASH diet recommends choosing whole grains over refined grains. Whole grains are high in fiber and other nutrients that help maintain healthy blood pressure.

3. Lean protein: The DASH diet recommends lean sources of protein, such as poultry, fish, beans, and nuts. These are lower in saturated fat and calories compared to red meats.

4. Low-fat dairy: The DASH diet recommends low-fat dairy products, such as milk, yogurt, and cheese. These are rich in calcium, vitamin D, and other nutrients.

5. Limited sodium: The DASH diet recommends limiting sodium to no more than 2,300 milligrams per day, or even less for some individuals.

6. Limited saturated fats: The DASH diet recommends limiting saturated fats to no more than 10% of daily calories.

7. Limited added sugars: The DASH diet recommends limiting added sugars to no more than 6 teaspoons per day for women and 9 teaspoons per day for men.

The Benefits of the DASH Diet

The DASH (Dietary Approaches to Stop Hypertension) diet has been consistently ranked as one of the healthiest diets by health professionals and nutrition experts. This diet focuses on consuming nutrient-rich whole foods and limiting processed and high-sodium foods. The DASH Diet is an excellent way to improve your overall health and prevent chronic diseases such as heart disease, diabetes, and high blood pressure.

Here are some benefits of the DASH diet in relation to this Cookbook:

1. Improves Heart Health: The DASH diet is well-known for its heart-healthy benefits. The diet promotes the consumption of foods rich in heart-healthy nutrients such as potassium, magnesium, and fiber. The recipes in this cookbook are designed to be low in sodium, saturated fats, and trans fats, making them ideal for people looking to improve their heart health.

2. Helps with Weight Loss: The DASH diet is an excellent diet for people looking to lose weight. The diet emphasizes the consumption of whole foods that are low in calories and high in nutrients, making them ideal for weight loss. The recipes in this cookbook are designed to be low in calories, making them ideal for people looking to lose weight.

3. Lowers Blood Pressure: High blood pressure is a risk factor for heart related disease and stroke. The DASH diet has been proven to lower blood pressure levels in people with hypertension. The recipes in this cookbook are designed to be low in sodium, making them ideal for people looking to lower their blood pressure levels.

4. Reduces the Risk of Chronic Diseases: The DASH diet is an excellent way to reduce the risk of chronic diseases such as heart disease, diabetes, and high blood pressure. The recipes in this cookbook are designed to be high in fiber, vitamins, and minerals, making them ideal for people looking to improve their overall health and reduce the risk of chronic diseases.

The benefits of the DASH diet are numerous and well-documented. The recipes in this cookbook are designed to help you achieve the benefits of the DASH diet in an easy and delicious way.

CHAPTER 2

Approved DASH Diet Guidelines for Healthy Weight Loss

This guide outline a verified DASH Diet guidelines for healthy weight loss

1. Control your calorie intake: To lose weight, you need to consume fewer calories than you burn. The DASH Diet recommends consuming between 1,200 to 1,500 calories per day, depending on your gender, age, and physical activity level. This cookbook provides recipes that are low in calories but still satisfying, so you can lose weight without feeling hungry.

2. Eat a variety of nutrient-dense foods: The DASH Diet encourages the consumption of fruits, vegetables, whole grains, lean proteins, and low-fat dairy products, which are rich in essential vitamins, minerals, and fiber. This cookbook provides a variety of recipes that incorporate these foods, making it easy to meet your daily nutrient needs.

3. Limit your sodium intake: The DASH Diet recommends limiting your daily sodium intake to no more than 2,300 milligrams, or 1,500 milligrams if you have high blood pressure or are at risk for it. This cookbook provides recipes that are low in sodium, making it easy to control your sodium intake.

4. Avoid processed and high-fat foods: Processed foods and foods high in saturated fats and added sugars can contribute to weight gain and other health problems. This cookbook provides recipes that use whole, natural ingredients, and limit the use of added sugars and saturated fats.

5. Practice portion control: Eating too much, even healthy foods, can still lead to weight gain. This cookbook provides recipes with appropriate portion sizes, so you can eat satisfying meals without overeating.

By following these guidelines, you can use this cookbook as a tool to achieve healthy weight loss while still enjoying delicious and nutritious meals.

CHAPTER 3

Approved DASH Diet Guidelines for Healthy Heart

The DASH diet is a dietary plan designed to help improve heart health and reduce the risk of heart disease. It focuses on consuming nutrient-rich foods while limiting the intake of saturated and trans fats, added sugars, and sodium. In this chapter, we will discuss the DASH diet guidelines for a healthy heart.

1. Consume More Fruits and Vegetables: The DASH diet encourages the consumption of fruits and vegetables, which are rich in vitamins, minerals, and fiber. This cookbook includes a variety of delicious DASH recipes that are rich in fruits and vegetables to help you meet your daily nutrient needs.

2. Choose Whole Grains: Whole grains provide fiber and other nutrients that are beneficial for heart health. This cookbook includes recipes that incorporate whole grains such as quinoa, brown rice, and whole wheat pasta.

3. Limit Saturated and Trans Fats: Saturated and trans fats can raise LDL (bad) cholesterol levels and increase the risk of heart disease. This cookbook focuses on using healthy fats such as olive oil and avocado instead of saturated and trans fats.

4. Choose Lean Protein Sources: This cookbook includes recipes that use lean protein sources such as fish, poultry, and legumes instead of high-fat meats.

5. Reduce Sodium Intake: Excessive sodium intake can increase blood pressure and increase the risk of heart disease. This cookbook provides low-sodium DASH recipes that are delicious and easy to prepare.

6. Moderate Alcohol Consumption: Moderate alcohol consumption can have some health benefits, but excessive alcohol intake can increase the risk of heart disease. This cookbook includes recipes for low-alcohol drinks that are suitable for people who want to limit their alcohol intake.

Following the DASH diet guidelines for a healthy heart can help improve heart health and reduce the risk of heart disease. This cookbook includes a variety of delicious DASH recipes that incorporate heart-healthy ingredients and nutrients to help you achieve your health goals.

How to Use This Cookbook

To make the most out of this cookbook, start by reading the DASH diet basics and guidelines for healthy weight loss and healthy heart. Take note of the ingredients and directions for each recipe, and plan your meals and snacks for the week ahead.

Use the provided meal planning templates to help you organize your meals and make grocery shopping easier. When cooking, be sure to measure ingredients accurately and experiment with herbs and spices for flavor.

Enjoy your meals mindfully and pay attention to how your body feels after eating. Track your progress by weighing yourself regularly and noting any changes in your health or energy levels.

Remember, the recipes in this cookbook are designed to help you achieve your weight loss and heart health goals, so choose the ones that appeal to your taste buds and dietary preferences. Have fun experimenting with different ingredients and flavors, and enjoy your journey towards a healthier, happier you!

CHAPTER 4

DELICIOUS DASH DIET RECIPES FOR WEIGHT LOSS AND HEALTHY HEART

Breakfast Recipes

#1. Oatmeal with Nuts and Berries

Servings: 2 | Prep time: 5 minutes | Cook time: 10 minutes

Ingredients:
- 1 cup old-fashioned rolled oats
- 2 cups water
- 1/4 cup chopped walnuts
- 1/4 cup fresh or frozen berries
- 1 tablespoon honey

Directions:

1. In a medium saucepan, bring the water to a boil.
2. Add the oats and reduce the heat to low. Cook for 5 minutes, stirring occasionally.
3. Remove from heat and stir in the walnuts and berries.
4. Drizzle with honey before serving.

Nutritional Info:
- Calories: 282

- Carbs: 45g
- Fat: 9g
- Protein: 8g
- Sodium: 5mg

#2. Whole Grain Toast with Avocado

Servings: 2 | Prep time: 5 minutes | Cook time: 5 minutes

Ingredients:
- 2 slices whole grain bread
- 1 avocado
- 1 tablespoon olive oil
- Salt and pepper to taste

Directions:
1. Toast the bread slices.
2. Cut the avocado in half and remove the pit.
3. Scoop out the avocado flesh and mash it in a small bowl.
4. Add the olive oil and mix well.
5. Spread the avocado mixture onto the toast.
6. Season with salt and pepper to taste.

Nutritional Info:
- Calories: 222
- Carbs: 20g
- Fat: 15g
- Protein: 5g
- Sodium: 224mg

Note: The nutrition information may vary depending on the specific brands of ingredients used.

#3. Veggie Omelette

Servings: 2 | Prep time: 10 minutes | Cook time: 10 minutes

Ingredients:
- 4 eggs
- 1/4 cup chopped onion
- 1/4 cup chopped bell pepper
- 1/4 cup chopped mushrooms
- 1/4 cup shredded cheddar cheese
- 1 tablespoon olive oil
- Salt and pepper to taste

Directions:
1. Beat the eggs in a small bowl and season with salt and pepper.
2. Heat the olive oil in a nonstick skillet over medium heat.
3. Add the onion, bell pepper, and mushrooms and sauté for 3-4 minutes.
4. Pour the eggs into the skillet and stir gently.
5. Sprinkle the shredded cheese over the top.
6. Use a spatula to fold the omelette in half.
7. Cook for 2-3 minutes until the cheese is melted and the eggs are cooked through.

Nutritional Info:
- Calories: 258
- Carbs: 6g
- Fat: 20g
- Protein: 15g
- Sodium: 282mg

#4. Greek Yogurt Parfait

Servings: 2 | Prep time: 10 minutes

Ingredients:
- 1 cup nonfat Greek yogurt
- 1/2 cup fresh berries (strawberries, blueberries, raspberries)
- 1/4 cup granola
- 1 tablespoon honey
- 1/4 teaspoon vanilla extract

Directions:
1. In a small bowl, mix together the Greek yogurt, honey, and vanilla extract.
2. In two serving glasses or jars, layer the yogurt mixture, berries, and granola.
3. Repeat the layers until the glasses or jars are full.
4. Serve immediately or store in the fridge until ready to eat.

Nutritional Info per serving:
- Calories: 200
- Carbs: 27g
- Fat: 2g
- Protein: 20g
- Sodium: 70mg

#5. Whole Grain Cereal with Almond Milk and Sliced Banana

Servings: 1 | Prep Time: 5 minutes

Ingredients:

- 1 cup whole grain cereal
- 1 medium banana, sliced
- 1 cup almond milk

Directions:

1. Add 1 cup of whole grain cereal in a bowl.
2. Over the cereal, pour 1 cup of almond milk..
3. Spread or top with sliced bananas.
4. Serve and enjoy!

Nutrition Info (per serving):

- Calories: 300
- Carbs: 55g
- Fat: 7g
- Protein:9g
- Fat: 7g
- Sodium: 200mg

Lunch recipes

#6. Grilled Chicken Salad

Servings: 4 | Prep Time: 20 minutes | Cook Time: 15 minutes

Ingredients:
- 4 boneless, skinless chicken breasts
- 8 cups mixed greens
- 1 cup cherry tomatoes, halved
- 1 avocado, diced
- 1/4 cup red onion, sliced
- 1/4 cup balsamic vinegar
- 2 tablespoons olive oil
- Salt and pepper to taste

Directions:
1. Preheat grill to medium-high heat.
2. Season chicken breasts with salt and pepper.
3. Grill chicken for 6-7 minutes per side, until fully cooked.
4. In a large bowl, mix together mixed greens, cherry tomatoes, avocado, and red onion.
5. In a separate bowl, whisk together balsamic vinegar, olive oil, salt, and pepper to make the dressing.
6. Slice the grilled chicken breasts and add to the salad.
7. Drizzle the salad with the dressing and toss to combine.

Nutritional Info:
- Calories: 296
- Carbs: 10g
- Fat: 14g
- Protein: 33g
- Sodium: 149mg

#7. Quinoa and Vegetable Stir-Fry

Servings: 4 | Prep Time: 10 minutes | Cook Time: 20 minutes

Ingredients:
- 1 cup quinoa
- 2 cups low-sodium vegetable broth
- 2 tablespoons olive oil
- 1 red bell pepper, sliced
- 1 green bell pepper, sliced
- 1 yellow onion, sliced
- 2 garlic cloves, minced
- 2 tablespoons low-sodium soy sauce
- 1 tablespoon honey
- 1 teaspoon ground ginger

Directions:
1. Rinse quinoa in cold water and drain.
2. In a medium-sized pot, bring the quinoa and vegetable broth to a boil.
3. Reduce heat to low and simmer for 15-20 minutes, until quinoa is cooked and fluffy.
4. In a large pan, heat olive oil over medium-high heat.
5. Add the sliced bell peppers, onion, and garlic to the pan and stir-fry for 5-7 minutes, until tender.
6. In a small bowl, whisk together soy sauce, honey, and ground ginger.
7. Add cooked quinoa to the pan with the vegetables and pour the sauce over the mixture.
8. Stir everything together until well combined.

Nutritional Info:
- Calories: 295
- Carbs: 41g
- Fat: 10g
- Protein: 10g
- Sodium: 167mg

#8. Turkey Wrap

Servings: 4 | Prep time: 10 minutes | Cook time: 5 minutes

Ingredients:
- 4 whole wheat tortillas
- 1 lb. turkey breast, sliced
- 1 avocado, sliced
- 1 tomato, sliced
- 1/2 red onion, sliced
- 1/4 cup plain Greek yogurt
- 1 tbsp. Dijon mustard
- 1 tbsp. honey
- Salt and pepper to taste

Directions:
1. In a small bowl, mix together Greek yogurt, Dijon mustard, honey, salt, and pepper.
2. Lay the tortillas out on a flat surface.
3. Spread the Greek yogurt mixture evenly over the tortillas.
4. Add sliced turkey, avocado, tomato, and red onion on top of the Greek yogurt mixture.
5. Roll up the tortilla tightly.
6. Serve immediately or wrap in plastic wrap and refrigerate until ready to serve.

Nutritional Info (per serving):
- Calories: 376
- Carbs: 26g
- Fat: 16g
- Protein: 33g
- Sodium: 190mg

#9. Greek Salad

Servings: 4 | Prep time: 15 minutes

Ingredients:
- 4 cups mixed greens
- 1/2 cup cherry tomatoes, halved
- 1/2 cucumber, sliced
- 1/2 red onion, sliced
- 1/2 cup kalamata olives, pitted
- 1/2 cup crumbled feta cheese
- 1/4 cup extra-virgin olive oil
- 2 tbsp. red wine vinegar
- 1 tsp. Dijon mustard
- Salt and pepper to taste

Directions:
1. In a large bowl, combine mixed greens, cherry tomatoes, cucumber, red onion, kalamata olives, and feta cheese.
2. In a small bowl, whisk together olive oil, red wine vinegar, Dijon mustard, salt, and pepper.
3. Pour the dressing over the salad and toss to combine.
4. Serve immediately.

Nutritional Info (per serving):
- Calories: 236
- Carbs: 10g
- Fat: 21g
- Protein: 4g
- Sodium: 282mg

#10. Lentil Soup

Servings: 4 | Prep time: 10 minutes | Cook time: 30 minutes

Ingredients:
- 1 cup dried green lentils, rinsed and drained
- 1 large onion, chopped
- 2 garlic cloves, minced
- 2 carrots, chopped
- 2 celery stalks, chopped
- 1 teaspoon ground cumin
- 4 cups low-sodium vegetable broth
- 1/4 cup chopped fresh parsley
- 1/4 cup chopped fresh cilantro
- Salt and pepper to taste

Directions:
1. In a large pot, heat 1 tablespoon of olive oil over medium heat.
2. Add the onion and garlic and sauté until the onion is translucent.
3. Add the carrots and celery and sauté for 5 minutes.
4. Add the lentils, cumin, and vegetable broth.
5. Bring to a boil, then reduce the heat to low and let simmer for 25 minutes or until the lentils are tender.
6. Remove from heat and stir in the parsley and cilantro.
7. Add salt and pepper to taste.

Nutritional Info (per serving):
- Calories: 191
- Carbs: 33g
- Fat: 1g
- Protein: 14g
- Sodium: 99mg

Dinner recipes

#11. Vegetable and Quinoa Stuffed Peppers

Servings: 4 | Prep Time: 20 minutes | Cook Time: 35 minutes

Ingredients:
- 4 bell peppers, halved and seeded
- 1 cup cooked quinoa
- 1 cup canned low-sodium black beans, drained and rinsed
- 1/2 cup corn kernels
- 1/2 cup chopped onion
- 1/2 cup chopped zucchini
- 1/2 cup chopped yellow squash
- 1/2 teaspoon ground cumin
- 1/2 teaspoon paprika
- 1/4 teaspoon garlic powder
- Salt and pepper to taste
- 2 tablespoons olive oil
- 1/4 cup chopped fresh cilantro

Directions:
1. Preheat oven to 375°F.
2. In a large bowl, combine quinoa, black beans, corn, onion, zucchini, yellow squash, cumin, paprika, garlic powder, salt, and pepper.
3. Brush the bell pepper halves with olive oil and fill each half with the quinoa mixture.

4. Place the stuffed peppers on a baking sheet and bake for 35 minutes or until the peppers are tender and the filling is heated through.
5. Garnish with cilantro and serve.

Nutritional Info (per serving):
- Calories: 231
- Carbs: 36g
- Fat: 7g
- Protein: 9g
- Sodium: 27mg

#12. Lemon and Herb Grilled Chicken

Servings: 4 | Prep Time: 10 minutes | Cook Time: 12 minutes

Ingredients:
- 4 boneless, skinless chicken breasts
- 1/4 cup lemon juice
- 1/4 cup olive oil
- 2 tablespoons chopped fresh rosemary
- 2 tablespoons chopped fresh thyme
- 2 tablespoons chopped fresh oregano
- Salt and pepper to taste

Directions:
1. In a small bowl, whisk together lemon juice, olive oil, rosemary, thyme, oregano, salt, and pepper.
2. Place the chicken breasts in a large resealable plastic bag and pour the marinade over the chicken.
3. Seal the bag and marinate in the refrigerator for at least 30 minutes or up to 4 hours.
4. Preheat grill to medium-high heat.

5. Remove the chicken from the marinade and discard the remaining marinade.
6. Grill the chicken for 6-7 minutes per side or until the internal temperature reaches 165°F.
7. Let the chicken rest for 5 minutes before slicing and serving.

Nutritional Info (per serving):
- Calories: 229
- Carbs: 2g
- Fat: 12g
- Protein: 28g
- Sodium: 97mg

#13. Baked Salmon with Asparagus

Servings: 4 | Prep time: 10 minutes | Cook time: 15 minutes

Ingredients:
- 4 salmon fillets
- 1 pound asparagus, trimmed
- 2 tablespoons olive oil
- 1 teaspoon garlic powder
- 1 teaspoon onion powder
- 1 teaspoon paprika
- Salt and pepper to taste

Directions:
1. Preheat oven to 400°F (200°C). Line a baking sheet with parchment paper.
2. Place the salmon fillets on the baking sheet and season with garlic powder, onion powder, paprika, salt, and pepper.

3. Drizzle olive oil over the salmon and asparagus.
4. Arrange the asparagus around the salmon on the baking sheet.
5. Bake for 15 minutes or until salmon is cooked through and asparagus is tender.
6. Serve and enjoy!

Nutritional Info:
- Calories: 280
- Carbs: 4g
- Fat: 19g
- Protein: 23g
- Sodium: 75mg

#14. Lentil and Vegetable Stir-Fry

Servings: 4 | Prep time: 10 minutes | Cook time: 30 minutes

Ingredients:
- 1 cup green lentils, rinsed and drained
- 2 cups water
- 1 tablespoon olive oil
- 1 onion, chopped
- 2 garlic cloves, minced
- 2 carrots, peeled and sliced
- 2 celery stalks, sliced
- 1 red bell pepper, sliced
- 1 teaspoon ground cumin
- 1 teaspoon ground coriander
- Salt and pepper to taste

Directions:

1. In a saucepan, bring water to a boil. Add lentils, reduce heat, and simmer for 20-25 minutes until tender. Drain any excess water and set aside.
2. Heat olive oil in a large skillet over medium-high heat. Add onion and garlic and sauté until fragrant.
3. Add carrots, celery, and bell pepper to the skillet and sauté until vegetables are tender.
4. Add cooked lentils, cumin, coriander, salt, and pepper to the skillet. Stir until well combined and heated through.
5. Serve and enjoy!

Nutritional Info:
- Calories: 260
- Carbs: 39g
- Fat: 4g
- Protein: 16g
- Sodium: 30mg

#15. Spicy Turkey Chili

Servings: 2 | Prep time: 10 minutes | Cook time: 30 minutes

Ingredients:
- 1 lb ground turkey
- 1 can (14.5 oz) low-sodium diced tomatoes
- 1 can (15 oz) low-sodium kidney beans, drained and rinsed
- 1 cup low-sodium chicken broth
- 1 onion, diced
- 1 red bell pepper, diced
- 2 cloves garlic, minced

- 1 tbsp chili powder
- 1 tsp ground cumin
- 1/4 tsp cayenne pepper
- Salt and pepper, to taste

Directions:
1. In a large pot, brown the ground turkey over medium-high heat. Drain any excess fat.
2. Add the onion, bell pepper, and garlic, and sauté until the vegetables are tender.
3. Add the diced tomatoes, kidney beans, chicken broth, chili powder, cumin, and cayenne pepper. Stir well to combine.
4. Bring the chili to a simmer, reduce heat to low, and let it cook for 20-25 minutes.
5. Season with salt and pepper to taste.
6. Serve hot and enjoy!

Nutritional Info per serving:
- Calories: 415
- Carbs: 35g
- Fat: 14g
- Protein: 38g
- Sodium: 209mg

Snack Recipes

#16. Avocado and Whole-Grain Crackers

Servings: 4 | Prep time: 10 minutes

Ingredients:

- 2 ripe avocados
- 1 lime, juiced
- 1/4 teaspoon salt
- Whole-grain crackers

Directions:

1. Cut the avocados in half, remove the pits, and scoop out the flesh into a bowl.
2. Add the lime juice and salt to the bowl and mash the ingredients together with a fork until it reaches your desired consistency.
3. Serve the avocado mixture with whole-grain crackers.

Nutritional Info (per serving):

- Calories: 230
- Carbs: 18g
- Fat: 18g
- Protein: 3g
- Sodium: 150mg

#17. Hummus and Vegetables

Servings: 4 | Prep time: 10 minutes

Ingredients:
- 1 can (15 ounces) low-sodium chickpeas, drained and rinsed
- 1/4 cup tahini
- 1/4 cup lemon juice
- 2 garlic cloves, minced
- 1/4 teaspoon salt
- Assorted chopped vegetables (such as carrots, cucumbers, and bell peppers)

Directions:
1. In a food processor, combine the chickpeas, tahini, lemon juice, garlic, and salt. Blend until smooth.
2. Transfer the hummus to a serving bowl and garnish with a drizzle of olive oil and a sprinkle of paprika.
3. Serve the hummus with chopped vegetables.

Nutritional Info (per serving):
- Calories: 180
- Carbs: 23g
- Fat: 8g
- Protein: 7g
- Sodium: 80mg

#18. Greek Yogurt with Berries

Servings: 4 | Prep Time: 5 minutes

Ingredients:
- 2 cups nonfat Greek yogurt
- 2 cups mixed berries (strawberries, blueberries, raspberries)
- 1 tablespoon honey
- 1/4 cup sliced almonds

Directions:
1. In a large bowl, mix the Greek yogurt and honey until well combined.
2. Divide the yogurt mixture into four bowls.
3. Top each bowl with mixed berries and sliced almonds.
4. Serve and enjoy!

Nutritional Info (per serving):
- Calories: 150
- Carbs: 18g
- Fat: 3g
- Protein: 16g
- Sodium: 50mg

#19. Apple and Almond Butter

Servings: 2 | Prep Time: 5 minutes

Ingredients:
- 1 medium apple, sliced
- 4 tablespoons almond butter
- 2 tablespoons unsweetened shredded coconut

Directions:
1. Place the apple slices on a plate.
2. Spread 2 tablespoons of almond butter over each apple slice.
3. Sprinkle the unsweetened shredded coconut on top of the almond butter.
4. Serve and enjoy!

Nutritional Info (per serving):
- Calories: 220

- Carbs: 15g
- Fat: 16g
- Protein: 6g
- Sodium: 50mg

#20. Roasted Chickpeas

Servings: 4 | Prep time: 5 minutes | Cook time: 30 minutes

Ingredients:
- 1 can (15 ounces) chickpeas, drained and rinsed
- 1 tablespoon olive oil
- 1 teaspoon paprika
- 1 teaspoon garlic powder
- 1/2 teaspoon cumin
- 1/4 teaspoon salt
- 1/4 teaspoon black pepper

Directions:
1. Preheat the oven to 400°F (200°C).
2. In a mixing bowl, combine the chickpeas, olive oil, paprika, garlic powder, cumin, salt, and pepper.
3. Spread the seasoned chickpeas in a single layer on a baking sheet.
4. Roast the chickpeas in the oven for about 30 minutes, or until crispy and golden brown.
5. Serve warm as a healthy snack or as a topping for salads.

Nutritional Info (per serving):
- Calories: 129
- Carbs: 17g
- Fat: 5g
- Protein: 6g
- Sodium: 273mg

#21. Grilled Peaches with Honey

Servings: 4 | Prep Time: 10 minutes | Cook Time: 10 minutes

Ingredients:
- 4 ripe peaches, halved and pitted
- 1 tablespoon honey
- 1 tablespoon olive oil
- pepper, to taste

Directions:
1. Preheat grill to medium-high heat.
2. Brush the cut side of each peach with olive oil and season with salt and pepper.
3. Place the peaches cut-side down on the grill and cook for 4-5 minutes until grill marks appear.
4. Flip the peaches over and grill for another 4-5 minutes until tender.
5. Drizzle honey over the peaches and serve.

Nutritional Info (per serving):
- Calories: 98
- Carbs: 20g
- Fat: 2g
- Protein: 1g
- Sodium: 0mg

#22. Chocolate Chia Pudding

Servings: 4 | Prep Time: 5 minutes

Ingredients:
- 1 cup unsweetened almond milk
- 1/4 cup chia seeds
- 2 tablespoons unsweetened cocoa powder
- 2 tablespoons maple syrup
- 1 teaspoon vanilla extract
- Fresh berries, for topping (optional)

Directions:
1. In a bowl, whisk together almond milk, chia seeds, cocoa powder, maple syrup, and vanilla extract.
2. Cover the bowl and refrigerate for at least 2 hours or overnight, until the pudding has thickened.
3. Divide the pudding into four serving glasses and top with fresh berries, if desired.

Nutritional Info (per serving):
- Calories: 130
- Carbs: 14g
- Fat: 7g
- Protein: 4g
- Sodium: 50mg

#23. Baked Apple with Cinnamon

Servings: 4 | Prep time: 10 minutes | Cook time: 30 minutes

Ingredients:
- 4 medium apples, cored
- 1 teaspoon cinnamon

- 1 tablespoon honey
- 1 tablespoon chopped walnuts

Directions:
1. Preheat oven to 375°F (190°C).
2. Place the apples in a baking dish.
3. Sprinkle cinnamon on top of the apples.
4. Drizzle honey over the apples.
5. Bake in the oven for 30 minutes or until the apples are tender.
6. Top with chopped walnuts and serve.

Nutritional info (per serving):
- Calories: 122
- Carbs: 32g
- Fat: 1g
- Protein: 1g
- Sodium: 1mg

#24. Poached Pears

Servings: 4 | Prep time: 10 minutes | Cook time: 20 minutes

Ingredients:
- 4 pears, peeled and cored
- 2 cups water
- 1 cup orange juice
- 1 cinnamon stick
- 2 cloves
- 1 teaspoon vanilla extract

Directions:
1. In a medium saucepan, combine the water, orange juice, cinnamon stick, cloves, and vanilla extract.
2. Bring to a boil.

3. Add the pears and reduce heat to low.
4. Simmer for 20 minutes or until the pears are tender.
5. Remove from heat and let cool.
6. Serve with the poaching liquid.

Nutritional info (per serving):
- Calories: 126
- Carbs: 33g
- Fat: 0g
- Protein: 1g
- Sodium: 6mg

#25. Berry Sorbet

Servings: 4 | Prep time: 5 minutes

Ingredients:
- 3 cups mixed berries (strawberries, raspberries, blueberries)
- 2 tablespoons honey
- 1 tablespoon fresh lemon juice

Directions:
1. Add the berries, honey, and lemon juice to a blender or food processor.
2. Blend until smooth.
3. Pour the mixture into a shallow container and freeze for 3-4 hours or until firm.
4. Scoop and serve.

Nutritional info (per serving):
- Calories: 89
- Carbs: 23g
- Protein: 1g
- Sodium: 2mg

Smoothie Recipes

#26. Berry Blast Smoothie

Servings: 2 | Prep time: 5 minutes

Ingredients:
- 1 cup mixed berries
- 1 banana
- 1 cup unsweetened almond milk
- 1 tsp honey

Directions:
Blend all ingredients until smooth and creamy.

Nutritional info (per serving): Calories: 155, Carbs: 35g, Protein: 3g, Fat: 2g, Sodium: 82mg, Sugar: 25g

#27. Green Apple and Spinach Smoothie

Servings: 2 | Prep time: 5 minutes

Ingredients:
- 2 cups spinach
- 1 green apple
- 1 banana
- 1 cup unsweetened almond milk
- 1 tsp honey

Directions:
Blend all ingredients until smooth and creamy.

Nutritional info (per serving): Calories: 156, Carbs: 35g, Protein: 3g, Fat: 2g, Sodium: 101mg, Sugar: 23g

#28. Peach and Carrot Smoothie

Servings: 2 | Prep time: 5 minutes

Ingredients:
- 2 cups chopped peaches
- 1 cup sliced carrots
- 1 banana
- 1 cup unsweetened almond milk
- 1 tsp honey

Directions:
Blend all ingredients until smooth and creamy.

Nutritional info (per serving): Calories: 175, Carbs: 40g, Protein: 3g, Fat: 3g, Sodium: 110mg, Sugar: 28g

#29. Pineapple and Kale Smoothie

Servings: 2 | Prep time: 5 minutes

Ingredients:
- 2 cups chopped kale
- 1 cup chopped pineapple
- 1 banana
- 1 cup unsweetened almond milk
- 1 tsp honey

Directions:
Blend all ingredients until smooth and creamy.

Nutritional info (per serving): Calories: 165, Carbs: 38g, Protein: 3g, Fat: 2g, Sodium: 116mg, Sugar: 24g

#30. Blueberry and Oat Smoothie

Servings: 2 | Prep time: 5 minutes
Ingredients:
- 1 cup blueberries
- 1 banana
- 1/2 cup rolled oats
- 1 cup unsweetened almond milk
- 1 tsp honey

Directions:
Blend all ingredients until smooth and creamy.

Nutritional info (per serving): Calories: 220, Carbs: 47g, Protein: 5g, Fat: 4g, Sodium: 117mg, Sugar: 22g

I hope you're enjoying Recipes in this Book! Would you like to experiment additional 60 Delicious DASH Diet Recipes for your Breakfast, Lunch, Dinner, Snack & Appetizers. Smoothies and even sweet Desserts.? I have a Complete Cookbook on that which you would enjoy in your weight loss journey. TO ACCESS THIS COOKBOOK, CLICK HERE

ACCESS THE DASH DIET COOKBOOK FOR BEGINNERS HERE

Final Thoughts and Testimony on the DASH Diet Eating Plan

The 30-day meal plan in **The Latest DASH Diet Cookbook for Beginners** was an enlightening experience. I learned all kinds of different flavors which I never knew existed and I appreciate the easy to follow format. This book guides one through an eating plan from shopping list to recipes, while stressing the importance of moving at a comfortable pace and making changes that will be for the long-term. As a stage 3 kidney patient, the DASH diet was highly recommended by my cardiologist, and the instructions in this book were clear, specific, and accurate. I was also able to learn how to mix and match foods and have the right portions so as not to exceed the daily calorie and sodium limit.

Overall, the 30-day meal plan on **The Latest DASH Diet Cookbook** was a great way for me to learn more about healthy eating, and I was able to make lasting lifestyle changes. I am now confident that I can continue to follow a DASH diet in the future and reap its many health benefits. I highly recommend this book to anyone looking to improve their eating habits and make healthier food choices.

- Debra C. Miller, London

BONUS: 30 DAY DASH DEIT MEAL PLAN FOR WEIGHT LOSS

Week 1 Meal Plan: Day 1-7

Day 1:

Breakfast: Recipe #2

Lunch: Recipe #7

Dinner: Recipe #12

Snack: Recipe #17

Dessert: Recipe #22

Smoothie: Recipe #27

Day 2:

Breakfast: Recipe #1

Lunch: Recipe #6

Dinner: Recipe #11

Snack: Recipe #16

Dessert: Recipe #21

Smoothie: Recipe #26

Day 3:

Breakfast: Recipe #5

Lunch: Recipe #10

Dinner: Recipe #15

Snack: Recipe #20

Dessert: Recipe #25

Smoothie: Recipe #30

Day 4:

Breakfast: Recipe #4

Lunch: Recipe #9

Dinner: Recipe #14

Snack: Recipe #19

Dessert: Recipe #24

Smoothie: Recipe #29

Day 5:

Breakfast: Recipe #3

Lunch: Recipe #8

Dinner: Recipe #13

Snack: Recipe #18

Dessert: Recipe #23

Smoothie: Recipe #28

Day 6:

Breakfast: Recipe #1

Lunch: Recipe #6

Dinner: Recipe #11

Snack: Recipe #16

Dessert: Recipe #21

Smoothie: Recipe #26

Day 7:

Breakfast: Recipe #5

Lunch: Recipe #10

Dinner: Recipe #15

Snack: Recipe #20

Dessert: Recipe #25

Smoothie: Recipe #30

Week 2 Meal Plan: Day 8-14

Day 8:

Breakfast: Recipe #1

Lunch: Recipe #6

Dinner: Recipe #11

Snack: Recipe #16

Dessert: Recipe #21

Smoothie: Recipe #26

Day 9:

Breakfast: Recipe #3

Lunch: Recipe #8

Dinner: Recipe #13

Snack: Recipe #18

Dessert: Recipe #23

Smoothie: Recipe #28

Day 10:

Breakfast: Recipe #2

Lunch: Recipe #7

Dinner: Recipe #12

Snack: Recipe #17

Dessert: Recipe #22

Smoothie: Recipe #27

Day 11:

Breakfast: Recipe #5

Lunch: Recipe #10

Dinner: Recipe #15

Snack: Recipe #20

Dessert: Recipe #25

Smoothie: Recipe #30

Day 12:

Breakfast: Recipe #3

Lunch: Recipe #8

Dinner: Recipe #13

Snack: Recipe #18

Dessert: Recipe #23

Smoothie: Recipe #28

Day 13:

Breakfast: Recipe #4

Lunch: Recipe #9

Dinner: Recipe #14

Snack: Recipe #19

Dessert: Recipe #24

Smoothie: Recipe #29

Day 14:

Breakfast: Recipe #2

Lunch: Recipe #7

Dinner: Recipe #12

Snack: Recipe #17

Dessert: Recipe #22

Smoothie: Recipe #27

Week 3 Meal Plan: Day 15-21

Day 15:

Breakfast: Recipe #3

Lunch: Recipe #8

Dinner: Recipe #13

Snack: Recipe #18

Dessert: Recipe #23

Smoothie: Recipe #28

Day 16:

Breakfast: Recipe #1

Lunch: Recipe #6

Dinner: Recipe #11

Snack: Recipe #16

Dessert: Recipe #21

Smoothie: Recipe #26

Day 17:

Breakfast: Recipe #4

Lunch: Recipe #9

Dinner: Recipe #14

Snack: Recipe #19

Dessert: Recipe #24

Smoothie: Recipe #29

Day 18:

Breakfast: Recipe #5

Lunch: Recipe #10

Dinner: Recipe #15

Snack: Recipe #20

Dessert: Recipe #25

Smoothie: Recipe #30

Day 19:

Breakfast: Recipe #2

Lunch: Recipe #7

Dinner: Recipe #12

Snack: Recipe #17

Dessert: Recipe #22

Smoothie: Recipe #27

Day 20:

Breakfast: Recipe #1

Lunch: Recipe #6

Dinner: Recipe #11

Snack: Recipe #16

Dessert: Recipe #21

Smoothie: Recipe #26

Day 21:

Breakfast: Recipe #5

Lunch: Recipe #10

Dinner: Recipe #15

Snack: Recipe #20

Dessert: Recipe #25

Smoothie: Recipe #30

Week 4 Meal Plan: Day 22-28

Day 22:

Breakfast: Recipe #1

Lunch: Recipe #6

Dinner: Recipe #11

Snack: Recipe #16

Dessert: Recipe #21

Smoothie: Recipe #26

Day 23:

Breakfast: Recipe #2

Lunch: Recipe #7

Dinner: Recipe #12

Snack: Recipe #17

Dessert: Recipe #22

Smoothie: Recipe #27

Day 24:

Breakfast: Recipe #3

Lunch: Recipe #8

Dinner: Recipe #13

Snack: Recipe #18

Dessert: Recipe #23

Smoothie: Recipe #28

Day 25:

Breakfast: Recipe #4

Lunch: Recipe #9

Dinner: Recipe #14

Snack: Recipe #19

Dessert: Recipe #24

Smoothie: Recipe #29

Day 26:

Breakfast: Recipe #5

Lunch: Recipe #10

Dinner: Recipe #15

Snack: Recipe #20

Dessert: Recipe #25

Smoothie: Recipe #30

Day 27:

Breakfast: Recipe #1

Lunch: Recipe #6

Dinner: Recipe #11

Snack: Recipe #16

Dessert: Recipe #21

Smoothie: Recipe #26

Day 28:

Breakfast: Recipe #3

Lunch: Recipe #8

Dinner: Recipe #13

Snack: Recipe #18

Dessert: Recipe #23

Smoothie: Recipe #28

Day 29:

Breakfast: Recipe #2

Lunch: Recipe #7

Dinner: Recipe #12

Snack: Recipe #17

Dessert: Recipe #22

Smoothie: Recipe #27

Day 30:

Breakfast: Recipe #5

Lunch: Recipe #10

Dinner: Recipe #15

Snack: Recipe #20

Dessert: Recipe #25

Smoothie: Recipe #30

CONCLUSION

Congratulations on taking the first step towards a healthier lifestyle with the DASH Diet. This cookbook has provided you with a variety of delicious and nutritious recipes that will help you achieve your weight loss and heart health goals.

As you embark on your journey, remember to keep the DASH Diet guidelines for healthy weight loss and healthy heart in mind, and use the tips provided in this cookbook to make meal planning and preparation easier.

Always strive to make small, sustainable changes in your diet and lifestyle, and don't be too hard on yourself if you slip up. Remember, it's about progress, not perfection.

In addition to the recipes in this cookbook, continue to explore new and healthy foods that you enjoy, and find ways to incorporate physical activity into your daily routine.

With determination and consistency, you may reach your health and fitness goals. Best of luck on your journey!

Thanks for reading my book! For more evidence-based nutrition books like this, please kindly check my amazon store at (https://www.amazon.com/author/alice-mcbride/). I will also appreciate you leave a nice review for me, just to help others out there make informed decision as yours. Thanks!

With love,

Alice McBride

Made in United States
Troutdale, OR
08/20/2023

12218289R00037